HOW WOULD YOU SURVIVE AS A

VIKING?

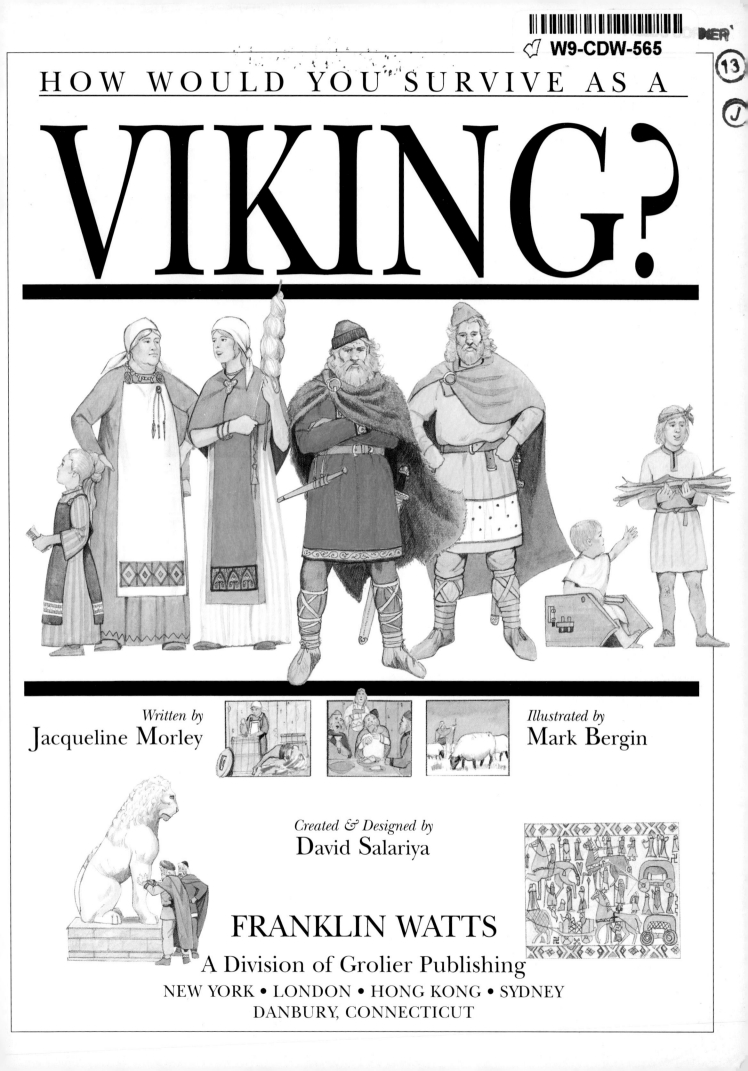

Written by
Jacqueline Morley

Illustrated by
Mark Bergin

Created & Designed by
David Salariya

FRANKLIN WATTS

A Division of Grolier Publishing

NEW YORK • LONDON • HONG KONG • SYDNEY

DANBURY, CONNECTICUT

David Salariya — *Director*
Diana Holubowicz — *Editor*
Dr. Richard Hall — *Consultant*

DAVID SALARIYA

was born in Dundee, Scotland, where he studied illustration and printmaking. He has illustrated a wide range of books on botanical, historical, and mythical subjects. He has created and designed many new series of books for publishers worldwide. In 1989 he established The Salariya Book Company. He lives in England with his wife, the illustrator Shirley Willis.

JACQUELINE MORLEY

is a graduate of Somerville College, Oxford. She has taught English and history, and now works as a freelance translator and writer. She has written historical fiction and nonfiction for children, and has a particular interest in the history of everyday life. She has also written **Entertainment** and **Clothes** in the *Timelines* series, **An Egyptian Pyramid** in the *Inside Story* series, and **How Would You Survive As an Ancient Egyptian?**

MARK BERGIN

studied illustration at Eastbourne College of Art. Since leaving art school in 1983, he has specialized in historical reconstructions and architectural cross sections. He has illustrated four titles in the award-winning *Inside Story* series and is a major contributor to the *Timelines* and *X-Ray Picture Book* series.

© THE SALARIYA BOOK CO LTD MCMXCIII

Printed in Belgium

Library of Congress Cataloging-in-Publication Data

Morley, Jacqueline.
How would you survive as a Viking? / written by Jacqueline Morley; illustrated by Mark Bergin; created and designed by David Salariya.
p. cm. – (How would you survive?)
Includes index.
ISBN 0-531-14344-9 (lib. bdg.) 0-531-15302-9 (pbk.)
1. Vikings – social life and customs – Juvenile literature.
2. Northmen – social life and customs – Juvenile literature.
[1. Vikings – social life and customs.] I. Bergin, Mark – ill.
II. Title. III. Series
DL65.M78 1995
948'.022 – dc20
94-26161
CIP AC
First American Edition 1995 by Franklin Watts
A Division of Grolier Publishing
Sherman Turnpike
Danbury, CT 06816
First Paperback Edition 1996

RICHARD A HALL BA PhD FSA MIFA

is deputy director of York Archaeological Trust. He has directed several large-scale excavations in York, including the internationally known Viking site at Coppergate. He is the author of *Viking Age Archaeology in Britain and Ireland* (1991) and *The Viking Dig* (1984), as well as archaeology reports and articles. He is a Fellow of the Society of Antiquaries of London, and a past chairman of the Institute of Field Archaeologists.

CONTENTS

BECOMING A VIKING. . .

4 Time Spiral

6 Basic Facts about Viking Life

8 Your Map of the Viking World

10 Begin Your New Life Here

14 **YOUR FAMILY**
WHERE DO YOU FIT IN?

15 **YOUR PLACE IN SOCIETY**
FREEMAN OR SLAVE?

16 **YOUR HOME**
WHERE WOULD YOU LIVE?

18 **FOOD**
WHAT WOULD YOU EAT?

20 **CLOTHES**
WHAT WOULD YOU WEAR?

22 **FARMING IN ICELAND**
HOW WOULD YOU LIVE AND WORK?

24 **LIFE IN A TOWN**
WHAT WOULD YOU FIND THERE?

26 **CRAFTS**
MAKING THE THINGS YOU NEED

28 **SHIPS**
HOW WOULD YOU SAIL?

30 **MERCHANTS**
WHAT CAN YOU SELL?

31 **RAIDERS**
WOULD YOU MAKE A FORTUNE?

32 **RIGHT AND WRONG**
WHO DECIDES?

34 **TRAVELING**
HOW WOULD YOU TRAVEL?

36 **RELIGION**
WHAT DO YOU BELIEVE?

38 **YOUR HEALTH**
HOW DO YOU KEEP CLEAN AND WELL?

40 **FROM CRADLE TO GRAVE**
BIRTH, MARRIAGE, AND DEATH

42 How Do We Know?

44 Timespan

46 Have You Survived?

47 Glossary

48 Index

SPIRAL

TIME

HERE IS THE AGE
OF THE VIKINGS

1953
Coronation of
Queen
Elizabeth II

Mount Everest
is conquered

Communist
leader Lenin
dies

1911
South Pole
conquered by
Amundsen

Titanic hits an
iceberg and
sinks

1700s
New farming
methods
introduced

1930
Mahatma
Gandhi's march

The age of
Hollywood

The Great
Depression
1929

1648
Taj Mahal
completed

1620
Mayflower sails
to America with
settlers

1454
Gutenberg
printing press
invented

1519
Cortés lands in
Mexico

2800 B.C.
Pyramids begin
to be built in
Egypt

1352 B.C.
Tutankhamen
dies

1952
Hydrogen bomb
tested

1066
William the
Conqueror
invades
England

850 B.C.
Assyrian Empire
established

691
Dome of the
Rock is built in
Jerusalem

1861
U.S. Civil War
begins

1935
Hitler becomes
führer of
Germany

1950
Korean War
breaks out

1951
Festival of
Britain

1750s
Industrial
Revolution

1660s
Invention of the
telescope and
microscope

1803
Napoleonic
Wars begin

1890s
Africa divided by
Imperial powers

1347
Onset of the
Black Death in
England kills
thousands

400s B.C.
Golden Age of
Greek
civilization

30
Crucifixion of
Christ

200
Rome repels
invaders

410
Fall of Rome

100,000 B.C.
Early man
hunting on the
plains of Africa

1364
Aztecs found
capital city,
Tenochtitlan

The Landscape

VAST MOUNTAINS divide the Scandinavian peninsula. Sweden, on its southeast, has fertile lowlands and vast forests that are rich in iron ore. In Norway, there are mountains that drop to the sea in many places, leaving only the narrow fjords and the river valleys for farming. Denmark's flatlands, in part bare wasteland, are split into many islands. Iceland is a bleak place to cultivate. It is for the most part treeless, stark, and barren.

The Homeland

AS A VIKING, you will not be able to go shopping for everything you need – there are no stores as we know them today. For food you will have to rely on what does well locally, and most of the things you use will have to be made from what is at hand. So your homeland is of vital importance to you. In cold, harsh Greenland you will have to manage very differently from the Danish Vikings who are much farther south.

The Seasons

YOU MAY FIND yourself living very far north, indeed. Because of the tilt of the globe, the regions near the poles have extreme variations in the length of night and day. At midsummer in Greenland and northern Scandinavia the sun never sets and in midwinter there is no daylight. In summertime you would have a very long workday, while in winter you would spend many weeks indoors, in almost total darkness.

Hunting & Fishing

IN THE MORE northerly Viking lands you will have to rely heavily on hunting and trapping to increase your food supply. You will find the sea teeming with many different kinds of fish; there are also whales and seals to be speared, and seabirds to be shot or snared and their eggs to be gathered. The rivers are full of salmon. In Scandinavia you would be able to hunt wild boar, red deer, and, in the far north, reindeer.

Viking Beliefs

UNTIL QUITE late in the Viking period (which lasted from the ninth century, when Vikings began raiding, to the eleventh, when they settled down), most Vikings were pagans. They worshiped gods belonging to the pagan past of the Germanic peoples. Some did convert to Christianity, yet they could still worship their pagan gods. Viking values may seem strange to you – they led hard lives and had no pity for weak people.

Viking Lifestyle

THE WORD "Viking" means piracy, or raiding. The Scandinavians had a terrifying reputation for this among their Christian and Slav neighbors. However, you will find that many Vikings have peaceable stay-at-home lives. Being born is one of the most dangerous stages of a Viking life. If you survive that, you can expect on average to live to about age fifty. Most Vikings are free, but you might be born as a slave.

The Wild Life

SUMMERTIME is short, and the winters are long and cold, though they may have been slightly milder in Viking times. The wild creatures around you, which are well adapted to these conditions, can be useful to you in a number of ways. The bear, the fox, and the marten will provide you with warm coats and coverings; the deer and the elk will provide you with meat. Furs and hides will also provide valuable goods to sell.

The Plants & Trees

YOU MAY BE LIVING near large areas of forest, especially in Norway and Sweden. If there is not enough farmland to support everyone, you may well have to cut down trees in order to create enough land to grow food. Trees are valuable. They give fuel for heating, cooking and metalworking, and timber to build houses and boats. If you cannot spare land for vegetables, you will have to go out and gather wild leeks and herbs.

Viking Farming

IN DENMARK and southern Sweden, your farm might be in a village. You would be able to grow wheat and barley, provided that the land is level and open. You would keep domestic animals, such as pigs and cattle, but would not have to rely on them as the northern Vikings must. Only grass grows really well in the far north. There you would lead an isolated life, for wide areas of pasture are needed to support the animals of even one family.

The Language

THE VIKINGS spoke what scholars today call Old Norse, the language from which modern Norwegian, Swedish, and Danish have developed. It varied little throughout Scandinavia. If you leave your Viking homeland, you will be able to talk to "foreign" Vikings quite easily. Modern English-speaking people would easily recognize some words; egg, skill, sky, and anger are just a few words the English learned from their Viking invaders.

Viking Names

MANY VIKING names are still in use today – Thora, Ingrid, Astrid, Olaf, Eric, and Harald, for instance. Animal names, Ulf (wolf), Bjorn (bear), were popular, and those like Thorvald or Thorkel, which referred to the thunder god Thor. The Vikings were very fond of nicknames: Harald Bluetooth, Ivar the Boneless, Radnor Lothbrok (hairy trousers), Thord the Short (he was very tall). What will they call you?

Viking Writing

THE SIGNS ABOVE spell the name Leif in Viking letters, which are called runes. The Vikings did not use pens. They cut the letters into wood. Runes were formed of straight strokes, as wood grain made curves hard to cut. Inscriptions in memory of people were cut on large stones. Here is the Viking alphabet. Choose your Viking name and see whether you can write it.

A	B	C	D	E	F	G	H	I	K	L	M

N	O	P	Q	R	S	T	U V W	X	Y	Z

YOUR MAP OF THE VIKING WORLD

NOW THAT YOU ARE a Viking, what part of the world will you be living in? That depends on when in the Viking story you arrive. Originally, the Vikings lived in the areas we now call Norway, Sweden, and Denmark. Many of their descendants still live in these countries today. But from the eighth to the eleventh centuries, Viking raiders, traders, and settlers made their way all over Europe and beyond. You might find yourself far from home for many months on a trading trip in Russia. In the ninth century you might be sailing with Vikings who made new homes in the Shetland Isles, the Orkneys, the Faroes, or Iceland, or fighting beside those who seized land in England, Ireland, or France. If you joined the tough fearless settlers who went to Greenland after 986, you might find yourself in America, nearly five centuries before Columbus got there.

THE VIKING VIEW OF THE WORLD
The Vikings will tell you that the earth is flat, and surrounded by an ocean in which the world serpent lies coiled. Beneath the earth is Hel, a dark and freezing place where the wicked go after their death.

THE RAINBOW makes a bridge to Asgard, the home of the gods. Viking poems describe how the ash tree, Yggdrasil, touches the heavens with its branches.
    One of its three roots grows beneath the earth, one reaches to Hel, and one to the mountains of the giants, which lie beyond the world's end.

WHERE YOU MIGHT LIVE

Homeland

Settlements

WHERE YOU MIGHT TRAVEL

Sea routes

Exploration and trade

WHERE YOU WOULD GET THINGS

Furs

Ivory

Timber

Gold

Pottery

Cloth

Weapons

Wine

Slaves

Amber

Spices

Silver

Fish

Silk

Fruit

Capstone

Salt

Wheat

Sheep (wool)

GREENLAND

ICELAND

FAROES

SHETLANDS

ORKNEYS

NORWAY

SWEDEN

DENMARK

ENGLAND

London

FRANCE

SPAIN

Rome

Staraja Ladoga

RUSSIA

Kiev

Bulgar

Constantinople

Baghdad

N

E

S

HERE AND ON the following pages is a panorama of the Viking world that awaits you. It is not meant to be a true-to-life picture, for you would not find all of these activities taking place at the same time. The panorama is your guide to this book. Start wherever you wish and follow the Q options.

BEGIN YOUR NEW LIFE HERE

WHY IS THIS shepherd taking his flock to the mountains? *Go to pages 22-23*

WHAT CROPS did the Vikings grow? To discover more about Viking farming, *Go to pages 22-23*

WHAT animals did the Vikings keep? *Go to page 18* How did they feed and look after them through the winter? *Go to pages 22-23*

HOW DID the Vikings keep themselves clean? *Go to pages 38-39*

HOW DID the Vikings make bread? What else did they eat? *Go to pages 18-19*

WHAT materials did the Vikings use to build their houses? How many rooms did they have and how did they use them? *Go to pages 16-17*

HOW DID the Vikings make cloth? *Go to page 26* What is this woman using to iron the clothes? *Go to pages 20-21*

WHAT WERE rune stones and what is this man doing?
Go to page 42
Did the Vikings have an alphabet?
Go to page 7

WHAT DID A blacksmith make and how did he work?
Go to page 26

WHAT DID Viking craftsmen make, and where would you expect to find their workshops?
Go to pages 24-25 and 26-27

THESE ARE iron furnaces. To find out what iron was used for,
Go to pages 26-27

WHAT WAS kept in storehouses? For just a few ideas,
Go to pages 16-17

WHO RULED the Viking world? What was the order of society?
Go to pages 14-15

WHAT WAS life like for Viking children? Did they go to school?
Go to pages 14-15

WHY DID some
Vikings
emigrate to new
lands? Where
might they be
going?
Go to pages 34-35

HOW DID the
Vikings worship
their gods? Why
is this person
kneeling before
a post, and what
is he hoping to
achieve? You
will find the
answers to these
questions on
pages 36-37

HOW DID the
Vikings keep
law and order?
To find out
about this and
to discover
what this man
is doing,
Go to page 33

WHAT DID the
Vikings believe
in? Did you
know that many
Vikings were
Christians? To
find out more,
Go to pages 36-37

WHAT TYPE of
cloth was for
sale and how
would it be
measured?
*Go to pages 20-21
and 26*

HOW FAR did
Viking traders
travel? What
did they buy
and sell, and is
this man for
sale?
Go to pages 30-31

WHAT TYPES of boats did the Vikings build? What were they made from and how? *Go to pages 28-29*

WHY WERE ships so important to the Vikings? *Go to pages 28-29* Where did the Vikings sail to in their ships? *Go to pages 30-31 and 34-35*

WHAT happened to the body of a dead Viking? To find out more about Viking burials, *Go to pages 40-41*

TO FIND OUT what happened when neighbors quarreled, *Go to page 32*

WHAT JOBS were carried out in winter? To find out about taking care of boats and other winter jobs, *Go to page 23*

WHY WAS the longboat such an outstanding vessel? *Go to page 28*

HOW DID Vikings organize their raiding parties and why did they take place? *Go to page 31*

YOUR FAMILY

WHERE DO YOU FIT IN?

FAMILY HONOR is very important. If a member is insulted by someone the entire family is offended. If one of them does something shameful the whole family is disgraced.

This wealthy man is setting off to see how his field-workers are doing with the harvest.

THIS IS WHAT YOUR FAMILY was like. You could count on its help in all life's difficulties. Vikings had a great sense of family loyalty. All the members looked after one another, so there were lots of aunts, uncles, and cousins around.

Your father might have been a freeman. He would have owned a farm and been a follower of a powerful earl. Your mother was an independent-minded woman, used to getting her own way. She had complete authority in household matters and would make all the decisions when your father was away. As the family was fairly prosperous, there were several free servants to help on the farm and in the house, and some slaves as well.

You and your brothers and sisters had to work hard. You did not go to school. There were no schools. Your parents taught you all the skills you needed in life.

A Scandinavian Viking family

He spends an hour teaching his son battle skills. He shows him how to ward off blows with his shield.

He speaks at the local Thing, an assembly that decides important local issues.

The women of the family wave good-bye as he and his companions set off on a raiding trip.

Q

If someone insulted your family, what could you do about it?
Go to page 32

CHILDREN ARE EXPECTED to show plenty of spirit. If you are strong-willed and quarrelsome, your parents will be pleased.

BY THE TIME you are twelve you will be ready to fend for yourself. At this age, Olaf, who was later king of Norway, joined a raiding expedition.

WOMEN MAY own property, but they may not sell it without their husband's consent. They may not vote at the Thing or conduct a lawsuit.

A WOMAN IN CHARGE

She directs the farm work while her husband is away from home.

She opens the storehouse where barrels of ale and meat are kept.

She orders a slave to take butter, cheese, and three cows to market.

Some suspicious characters are seen. She leads an attack on them.

She directs the women workers as they prepare the evening meal.

Afterward, everyone gathers around as she tells a story by the fire.

YOUR PLACE IN SOCIETY
F R E E M A N O R S L A V E ?

Dawn. The first job is to check that the fire has not gone out.

THE KING WAS THE most important person in the region. He was the leader of the great landowners, or earls, who obeyed him. These earls were themselves supported by the freemen of the neighborhood. The freemen were both farmers and warriors, for all free Vikings knew how to handle weapons. They fought for their chief in his feuds and went with him to war. He helped them in their disputes and rewarded them generously.

When they made raids together, he shared the spoils. If you were forceful and had some land, you could recruit a band of followers, vow to protect them, and so become a chief yourself.

An earl

Next, the animals must be fed, and the stables and cow barns cleaned.

A freeman

At mealtimes the slaves eat at the far end of the table.

A slave

IF YOU ARE A SLAVE, you face a life of hard work. You cannot own land, carry weapons, or vote at the Thing. Your owner might give you your freedom, or allow you to buy it with extra work. Then you could become a free servant or a craftsman.

A slave sleeps wherever he can – on the floor, or with the animals.

Q

What might you get as a reward for serving your warlord?
Go to page 21

What would life be like as a farmer?
Go to page 22

THE LIFE OF A KING

A king must have royal blood and the support of the chiefs he rules over.

He rewards his loyal followers with gifts of gold and silver and land.

Missionaries want to build a church. The king consults the Thing about this.

The king visits the most powerful earls to discuss plans for defense.

An earl in charge of a frontier region brings news of enemy invasion.

Death in battle. "Kings are made for honor not for long life."

YOUR HOME

WHERE WOULD YOU LIVE?

THIS IS A farmhouse in Iceland. Workrooms and storerooms open off the main living area. There would be stables, barns, and a smithy nearby.

Holes are dug for the four stout corner posts. These are braced with strong cross timbers.

The gable ends are set up. Lighter timber is used for the roof ridge and supports, and the wall posts.

Thin rods are set between the wall posts, leaving a gap for the door. Wattles (hazel canes) are woven through them.

The roof is thatched with straw, reeds, or heather, and the floor is made of beaten earth.

Right: Some every-day things you might use at home.

YOUR HOUSE WAS probably built of wood, provided that the winters were not too cold. In places like Iceland where there are fewer trees, or Greenland where there are none, you would have had to build your house from stones and turf, which would be better at keeping out the cold. The timbers of a wooden house were usually set directly into the ground and tended to rot. After twenty years or so, there was a lot of repair work to do. The roof, which was thatched with straw or reeds, needed patching even sooner. You and your family lived, ate, and slept in one big room. There was a stone-lined hearth in the center, where meals were cooked. Smoke found its way out through the doorway or through a gap at the top of the gable wall. The odors of people and cooking had to escape that way as well, for there were no windows to open. Low platforms along both long walls provided draft-free areas for sitting and for sleeping. You certainly had almost no privacy!

THE WALLS OF a turf house were built up of layers of turf laid on a stone foundation. Wood was only used for roof supports and for inside partitions and paneling. The roof was covered with thinner turf.

Smithy

Outdoor lavatory

A baby's chair, made of slotted wooden planks.

A baby's wooden, feeding bowl, with handle and spout.

A bucket made from wooden staves, with carrying handles.

Stone lamp. Whale oil or animal fat is burned in it.

An oak storage chest strengthened with iron bands.

Q

What is booty, and where could you steal it from?
Go to page 31

Why is there a cow over the doorway of this house? See page 36 for the answer.

Loom

Quern (hand mill)

Drying fish

Pathway of split logs

SMALLER BUILDINGS near the house are used as workrooms, store-houses, and sheds for the animals. Even if you live in a town, you will keep pigs and hens, and perhaps a goat.

YOU CAN MAKE a small house quickly and economically by digging a pit and roofing it over, as the Slavs do. You will need two props and a cross-piece to hold up the roof. You may be quite snug if the soil is dry.

You did not need very much furniture. Your bed was made up directly onto the platform by the wall. Your parents might have had a regular bed, perhaps in a partitioned-off cubicle if the house was large enough.

There was a table and stools. Rich homes had cushions and wall hangings as well, and the head of the family might have had a special "high seat" with tall decorated side posts. Your mother's loom took up quite a lot of room, but apart from these items, and some cooking jars and pans, the rest of the furniture was for storage. Food was stored in barrels of various sizes, and clothes and valuables were kept in chests.

Q

If you wanted to divorce your husband, what could you do?
Go to page 41

Why would you want to become Christian?
Go to pages 36-37

MAKING WATTLE AND DAUB

To make wattle and daub, hazel bushes are coppiced (pruned back).

Then they grow many thin stems. The thicker ones are split.

The hazel is woven in and out between strong poles.

Mud is plastered over, to make the wall draft proof.

To make a well, you dig down to reach the groundwater.

An old barrel, or planks, are used to line the well.

Reed makes the best thatch, and it is your first choice if it grows nearby. You may have to use straw or heather instead.

The reeds are harvested from the banks of lakes and rivers and sorted into bundles for the thatcher.

He sets bunches of reeds side by side in rows over planks, starting from the bottom of the roof.

Each row is held in place by thin lengths of split hazel, fastened down with bent hazel twigs.

F O O D

WHAT WOULD YOU EAT?

THIS WAS HOW YOU would have cooked your food. But where would you have gone to buy your food? Unless you happened to live in a town where there was a market, you would have had to grow your own food on your land and pick the things that you found growing wild in the forests and the land around your dwelling. You would have had to keep animals such as pigs, goats, and cows and kill them yourself if you wanted to eat meat. The Vikings liked to eat plenty of it! Hunting and fishing were not just sports – they were also an essential source of food. The most important elements in a Viking's diet, such as fruit, berries, meat, and fish, are shown on this page.

Fruit and nuts

Beef   *Venison*

Mutton

Pork

Whale meat

Herring

Seal

Salmon

Q

You thought you'd be dining on your own. Why have lots of people turned up to share your meal?
Go to page 32

BREAD-MAKING

First you have to make flour by grinding wheat or barley in a quern (hand mill) made from two stones.

The top stone turns on the bottom one and crushes the grain. Then you mix the flour with water to make dough.

The dough is mixed in a long wooden trough. Some raw dough saved from the last baking day is added.

This has live yeast in it which makes the bread rise. The dough has to be kneaded to help it rise.

The risen dough is shaped into loaves and left to rise again. Now it is ready to be baked.

Each loaf is set over the fire on a long-handled griddle. It will bake slowly over the hot ashes.

Preparing the food was a job done by the women of the family. If you were a girl, you helped your mother almost from the time you started to walk. She would get you to stir the porridge and collect the eggs from under the hens, and send you out to look for wild leeks, mushrooms, and strawberries. As you grew older, you learned to make bread, churn milk into butter, make sour-milk cheese, brew ale, wring a chicken's neck and pluck it, gut and smoke fish, and help with all the salting and pickling of meat that had to be done in the autumn, when many of the cattle were killed.

If yours was a rich family, the women servants served the food at mealtimes, and filled up the tankards and drinking horns, perhaps with wine instead of ale. People used knives to cut their food, and ate it with their fingers or with a spoon if necessary.

Bowls are not always made of pottery. It can be easier to make them of soapstone, like the one above.

Two frying irons with revolving cooking surfaces (**a**,**b**), a ladle (**c**), a toaster (**d**), and a fork (**e**) for skewering meat.

Striking a light. A steel striker (above) is struck on a flint to make sparks (right).

Wooden troughs are carved at home. Someone has enjoyed decorating these ends, shown in detail.

A bucket made of wooden staves banded with iron. Its wide base makes it less easy to knock over.

COOKING MEAT

Most meat is grilled or roasted. How would you cook a very big piece of meat?

Dig a pit in the ground and line it with wood. Meanwhile, some large stones heat on the fire.

Fill the pit with water and lower the joint of meat into it. Add salt and herbs for a good flavor.

Drop hot stones into the pit, to bring the water to boil. A 10-pound (4.5-kg) joint cooks in three hours.

You could also bake food in a hole packed with hot embers and covered with earth to keep in the heat.

The best meat is roasted on a spit. You have to turn the spit fairly often to cook the meat evenly.

Q

Where could you get a new pair of soft leather shoes?
Go to page 27

What could you do in the evenings after supper?
Go to page 14

CLOTHES
WHAT WOULD YOU WEAR?

First she pulls on a finely pleated linen petticoat with wide, loose sleeves. This reaches her feet.

Then she adds a shorter, open-sided overdress and fastens its straps with large oval brooches.

Over this, she puts a long woolen shawl, which she pins together at her throat with a third big brooch.

Y OU NEEDED really warm clothes for the Scandinavian climate, at least for most of the year. You might be a farmer outdoors in all weather, or a merchant battling with wind and rain on land or at sea. Even stay-at-home townsmen and womenfolk had to fetch water, chop wood, pen animals, and do all sorts of other outdoor jobs in ice and snow. Your clothes would almost all be home-made, either by you or your servants.

What could you use to make your clothes? Your sheep provided wool from which to make warm cloth. This was a lengthy process, which occupied the women of the household for much of the year. If you could get to a large market, you could buy very fine woolen cloth imported from Frisia and silk from the Far East, but these were very expensive.

The tough fibers of the flax plant were spun and woven into linen for underclothes. This was hard work, for the flax had to be well beaten first, to make the fibers fit for use. For waterproof protection, you needed animal skins, and for real warmth, furs.

You will want to decorate your clothes with bands of patterned ribbon. See page 26 to find out how these are made.

How will you iron your clothes? The whalebone board and the heated glass ball shown (below right) could be an ironing board and iron.

BUSY HOUSEWIVES and mothers need clothes that are practical. The loosely hanging over-tunic and pleated linen petticoat can easily be drawn aside when your baby needs to be breast-fed.

Women tie their hair in a knot at the nape of the neck. Some wear eye makeup. After you are married, you will usually keep your hair covered.

A necklace of carnelian and crystal beads, hung with trinkets brought back from the Far East.

Luxurious gold buckle. Most brooches are of silver or copper alloy.

An oval dress buckle. These varied a lot in quality. You will want to wear the best you can afford.

Nail cleaner and ear scoop. They were worn hanging from women's brooches, like keys.

This is how you would be dressed as a prosperous married woman. You have fine jewelry and your overdress is richly decorated with a woven panel.

Q
How did Vikings get hold of cloth and silk from the East?
Go to page 30

How to copy a brooch cheaply, using very little metal? Make a baked-clay mold of the face of the brooch.

Line it with cloth dipped in clay. Press more clay against it to form the back of the mold.

Separate the pieces and remove the cloth. This leaves a thin gap into which molten metal can be poured.

There is no soap.
Ammonia from
cows' urine is used.
It is a good cleaning
agent.

Clothes are washed
in running water or
rinsed in ammonia.

You were glad to have leggings
and long skirts. Viking houses
could be both stuffy and drafty.
Women wore knee-length cloth
leggings under their skirts in
cold weather. Both men and
women wore heavy cloaks and
fur wraps for winter. No matter
how cold the weather was, you
always pinned your cloak so that
your sword arm was uncovered
and you could reach your sword
at a moment's notice.

A man's massive
neck-ring made of
almost 4 lb (2 kg) of
gold. It might be
your reward for
serving your warlord.

Long leggings are
worn under the
tunic. They can be
tight, or loose like
trousers, in which
case you might bind
them to your legs
with bands of cloth
or leather.

Three-lobed
brooches, often
worn at the neck,
are popular.

Shoes are made of
leather. Some
winter shoes have
the hair left on them
for extra warmth.
This winter ankle
boot might be
worn for
skating.

Slaves and poor
people wear plain,
rough woolen
tunics. They tie
cloth or skins
around their feet
for shoes.

THIS RICH VIKING merchant has
traveled abroad. His clothes are
influenced by the styles of the Slav
peoples of central Europe. He has
a fur-trimmed hat and enormously
wide trousers bound tightly to his
legs below the knees. His cloak is
fastened with a big ring-and-pin
brooch.

VIKING CHILDREN wear clothes
in very much the same style as their
parents'. Girls wear pinafore
dresses like their mothers', and
boys wear leather or woolen
jerkins and leggings. Indoors, they
wear soft leather shoes or sandals.
Outside they wrap up in warm
woolen cloaks and boots. Rich
children have fur-lined cloaks and
fur hats and mitts.

Q

How would you
make wool into
cloth?
Go to page 26

How would you
keep yourself
clean?
Go to pages 38-39

FARMING IN ICELAND

HOW WOULD YOU LIVE AND WORK?

A S A VIKING FARMER you had to make your land provide the best living for your family. If you lived in Scandinavia, there was enough sunshine to grow oats and barley, and perhaps some rye and wheat. You could keep enough livestock for your own needs and use the rest of your land to grow cereals to sell.

But suppose you lived in Iceland, where oats and barley grow with difficulty, or Greenland, where they will not grow at all? Then you had to live off the grasslands.

This meant relying on hunting and fishing and on rearing cattle and sheep. These animals needed plenty of pasture, so you needed more land than the southern Vikings did.

The year begins in April, when the snow melts. It is time for plowing and for sowing the barley and oats.

In early spring, the walls around the home-meadow are repaired, where frost has damaged them.

Toward the end of May, the lambs are old enough to be taken from their mothers. The adult sheep are shorn of their fleece.

Along the coast, May and June are the time for gathering eggs from millions of seabirds that nest on the cliffs.

Q

Where can you get a new set of knives made?
Go to page 26

If you were a farmer and there was no land to spare, what could you do?
Go to pages 34-35

IN THE SUMMER, some of the family stay at the shieling, a small house in the mountains. They take the herds there to find better grass.

At the shieling in midsummer, the animals yield lots of milk. Butter and curd cheeses are made.

The dairy produce is sent to the coast on packhorses, where it will be sold, or traded for salt or fish.

August is hay-making month. Not only the hay meadow but every small patch of long grass is cut.

In late August and early September, the corn is cut. The cattle are allowed to eat the remaining stubble.

In October the herds are rounded up in readiness for winter. Some may have strayed many miles.

Fuel has to be laid in for the long dark winter months. Trees are felled and slabs of peat are cut.

The first settlers in Iceland claimed so much land that there was often little left for latecomers. Even so, your farm was isolated. The best site was at the foot of the mountains, and close to the lowland. There you had shelter from the harsh winters and easy access to the mountain grass in summer.

Claiming your land. A man is allowed as much land as he can walk around in a day, carrying a torch. A woman has to drive a cow along with her.

In the morning you drive the boar to the home meadow to fatten. He alone is allowed to eat the best grass.

You have to supervise the housework, the pigs, and poultry. Today, there is fish to cook, gut, and dry as well.

Weaving takes all your spare time. Cloth is one of the few things Icelanders can offer foreign traders.

Grass grows on the turf roof

Your farmhouse was built of turf, on a stone base, and the rooms were lined with wood. The long main room had several others opening from it. These could serve as bedrooms or weaving rooms, or they might house the dairy or toilet. You also needed warm houses for the animals in winter, barns to store hay, and a smithy. These were grouped around the farmhouse. In front of the farm was the home meadow, which was walled to prevent the animals from eating its carefully tended grass. It was the main source of hay, which kept the cattle alive in winter.

In the evening you do the milking. At busy times, like hay-making, you have to work hard in the fields.

Q

You've got a juicy joint of meat from the autumn slaughter. How will you cook it? *Go to page 19*

What rights do women have? *Go to page 14*

Some animals have to be killed each autumn. There is not enough hay for them all. The meat is packed in salt.

This is the time for having feasts and celebrating weddings, for there is plenty of fresh meat to eat.

Animals cannot spend winter nights outdoors, but in the day sheep and goats nibble grass through the snow.

Cows are more delicate. They are kept in barns, called byres, day and night in winter and fed there.

The long dark winter is the time for indoor work, like making and mending tools, and repairing boats.

Animal skins from the autumn slaughter are made into warm clothing, shoes, and bed covers.

LIFE IN A TOWN
WHAT WOULD YOU FIND THERE?

*King Godfred of
Denmark destroyed
the Slav town of
Reric and moved its
traders to a site at
Hedeby in 808.*

*A missionary,
Anskar, came to
Hedeby in around
830 and was allowed
to build a church. He
did not make many
converts.*

*In the tenth century
King Harald
Bluetooth built a
rampart around the
town to protect it
from attack.*

*In 1050 the town
was burned by
Norwegian Vikings.
Sixteen years later it
was destroyed by a
Slav people, the
Wends.*

Q

Why would
anyone want to
colonize a
remote place
like Staraja
Ladoga?
Go to page 30

THERE WERE many advantages to town life. You would not have had complete control over your food supply, since much that you needed came from the country, but this was only a drawback in times of famine. You found plenty of country people in the market, wanting to sell you food. Towns were, above all, places where people met to do trade. This was how towns came into being in the first place. At Hedeby, for instance (today in Northern Germany), you met merchants of all kinds – some with amber and furs from the Northern Baltic, others from Norway and Sweden with soapstone bowls, reindeer hides, and cargoes of bog iron. There were also Frankish traders with fine goldsmith's work, cloth merchants from Frisia (modern Netherlands), and some adventurous traders who came north through Russia, bringing silks and spices and looking for slaves.

If you were a craftsman hoping to earn a good living, the town was the place to be. Craftsmen's workshops lined the streets, with goods set out to catch the eye of wealthy passersby.

TOWNS often
have a mint,
authorized by
the king to issue
coins. Above
are two silver
coins made at
Hedeby.

Whale being gutted

Merchants' tents

*Most houses have
a fenced-off patch
of land.*

*These fish are
being dried for
storing.*

*Some houses have
outdoor toilets.
Refuse is buried or
goes in the stream.*

*The stream flows
through the middle
of the town. It is a
convenient place for
doing the washing.*

THIS IS the town of Staraja Ladoga. Although it is far away in northern Russia, the land of the Finns and Slavs, some of it has been built by Vikings. They come mostly from Sweden and find it convenient to have a base here.

Farmers meet to buy and sell livestock. They bring surplus butter, cheese, and grain to sell in the market.

Towns were encouraged and protected by ambitious kings. In return for protecting its inhabitants and for allowing the market to be held, a king received a proportion of the profits made there – a tax, in fact. Kings needed plenty of money to pay their followers and keep their power. As one of the townspeople, you would have benefited from the arrangement. A town without the backing of an army was at the mercy of sea pirates (possibly Vikings from other regions!) or foreign invaders, while a well-defended one attracted merchants from far and near and became more and more prosperous.

THIS IS a view of Hedeby looking toward the harbor. The wall extends into the water to make a safe haven. Some visiting merchants have pitched tents by the shore.

Godfred sited his new town where the route used by merchants from the south met those of sea traders from east and west.

You can buy shoes, saddlery, weapons, jewelry, and tools from the craftsmen's market stalls.

Merchant ships

Merchants bring goods from afar: swords, glass, wine, and silk from the south; ivory, furs, and slaves from the north.

In the slave market you will be sold Christians. They are hard to sell abroad. Other Christians will not deal in them.

Q

You want to have a steam bath. How can you do this?
Go to page 38

There are plenty of country sights and smells in the town. People keep pigs and poultry and even cows in their backyards.

Hedeby is a large town by Viking standards. This view shows only a section. Many houses have storage sheds and workshops alongside.

If you want a high-quality sword that will not bend, you must go to a smith who knows the art of damascening.

He will heat iron rods until their surface turns to steel, and then twist several rods together to join the steel and iron.

When the metal is hammered, the iron and paler steel form a pattern. Such a blade deserves a finely decorated hilt.

C R A F T S
MAKING THE THINGS YOU NEED

MANY OF THE THINGS that you used were homemade. You were expected to know how to use your hands. The men of the household knew how to fell trees, cut up the timber, and shape it into gates and fences, tools, carts, sleds, and furniture.

Many farmers had their own smithies, where they made and mended iron tools and vessels. You needed these skills if you lived in a remote area. Where farms were reasonably close together, you might be visited by a traveling blacksmith.

Part of a piece of tapestry. Wealthy Vikings hang tapestry on their walls for warmth.

The warp threads, kept taut by hanging weights, are separated into two layers, one attached to the heddle bar. By moving the bar, you lift alternate layers and pass the weft thread between them.

The smith works iron by heating and hammering it. His assistant raises the heat of the fire with bellows.

He makes all the iron products that you need: knives, axes, cooking pans, keys, and padlocks like the one shown above.

Skilled smiths specialize in decorative work. This ax is being prepared to take an inlay of contrasting metal.

The pattern is marked on the iron blade in grooves. Silver wire is then hammered into the grooves.

All women are trained in a craft, for they are the cloth makers. Even in the wealthiest families girls are taught to spin and weave. For most women carding, spinning, weaving, dyeing, cutting, and stitching make a never-ending job. They not only clothe the family but produce bedclothes, wall hangings, and sails for the ships.

Cloth-making tools:
a. iron-toothed comb for disentangling the fibers of the sheep's clipped fleece;
b. cutting shears;
c. reel onto which newly-spun thread is wound.

a

b

c

Loom weights

WOMEN'S CRAFTS

Viking women are skilled embroiderers. Patterned braid is woven by passing warp threads of various colors through holes in a series of wooden or antler tablets.

To work, the weaver ties one end of the work around her waist, and the other end to something fixed. She twists the tablets to vary the warp positions and produce the design.

This woman is pushing the weft into place. Her companion spins from a distaff.

Cloth is sold in body measurements. An ell, for instance, is the length from your elbow to your fingertips. Don't buy from someone with short arms!

MAKING JEWELRY

Brooches are made by pouring molten bronze or pewter into molds. This is a mold of carved soapstone.

A pendant decorated with filigree. If you buy it, ask if it is pure gold or silver or only coated.

Filigree patterns are made of wire that has been melted in a heated mold to form a string of tiny beads.

MAKING AN ANTLER COMB

Use the antler of the red deer. This makes a strong comb. Cut a piece to the length of comb you want.

From this, cut two long plates to form the comb's back. These can be ornamented with a pattern of carved lines.

Bone carvers sell many small decorative objects. This figure is a playing piece for a board game.

Useful things made from bone: **a**. a name tag marked in runes; **b**. a comb (with some teeth missing); **c**. a pin.

Now cut a series of small plates from spare pieces of antler. These will form the teeth of the comb.

Drill holes in the plates and the back pieces. Assemble the comb and secure it with small iron pins.

If you wanted something out of the ordinary, perhaps to give as a present – a silver brooch, a bead necklace, or a decorated sword – you had to go to a town. There you could see these things being made by craftsmen who sold them from their workshops. You could watch them carving bone, amber, and jet, and making multicolored beads by fusing fragments of different colored glass. If you preferred a quiet steady life to a risky one, you might decide to make a living as a craftsman.

A bone carver. He sells his goods directly from his work stall.

Now that the small plates are securely held, you will find it easy to saw each into several teeth.

OTHER CRAFTSMEN

Leather workers supply things that need to be tough yet pliable, like shoes, belts, and harnesses. Fine items often have raised designs on them. This is called embossing.

Soapstone, a soft rock that is found in natural outcrops, has many uses. The required shape is cut in the rock face and detached by undercutting.

The craftsman may take the soapstone piece home to finish. He makes lamps, cooking pots, bowls, loom weights, and molds for metal casting.

S H I P S

CONSTRUCTING A LONGBOAT

A SKILLFUL SHIPBUILDER watches growing trees and notes those which will give the shapes he needs. Oak logs are split into wedge-shaped pieces to provide planks. Pine is split vertically and gives fewer logs.

THE KEEL, which is the ship's backbone, is laid down first. Curved stems at each end form the prow at the front of the ship and sternpost at the rear. They are attached to the keel by overlapping joints.

NEXT THE SIDES ARE built up of long planks, known as strakes. Each is specially shaped to suit its place in the vessel. When the shell of the boat is complete, inner ribs and crosspieces are added for strength.

THE STRAKES ARE JOINED with iron nails, backed with a roving (metal plate). Caulking, made of tarred wool; is packed between the strakes to make them watertight. Oar holes are cut and given pivoting covers.

THE SHIP IS GUIDED by a rudder like a large paddle, which is attached to the stern on the starboard, or right side. The bottom of the mast is held steady by a huge block of wood known, from its shape, as the mast fish.

IF YOU WERE ASKED what you most longed to own, as a Viking you would almost certainly reply "a really fine ship." Vikings were justifiably proud of their skills in shipbuilding and seamanship. They were famous throughout the northern seas for making boats that were exceptionally swift and strong, yet supple enough to withstand the battering of ocean waves, and also shallow enough to travel far inland along rivers. Sailing was part of daily life. Not knowing how to sail was even more of a disadvantage to a Viking than not knowing how to drive a car today.

Your father would have taught you how to row and to handle the sail of a small boat when you were very young.

If you wanted anything better than a rough workboat, you went to a professional shipbuilder. He showed you his timber, sometimes stored underwater to prevent warping, and told you that the best ships were made of oak. He might use pine or birch instead, but the keel, or backbone of the ship, which gives the ship its strength, was always made of oak.

Knorr

The knorr is a sturdy cargo boat built to withstand rough seas. The riverboat is a small workboat that can hoist a sail.

Riverboat

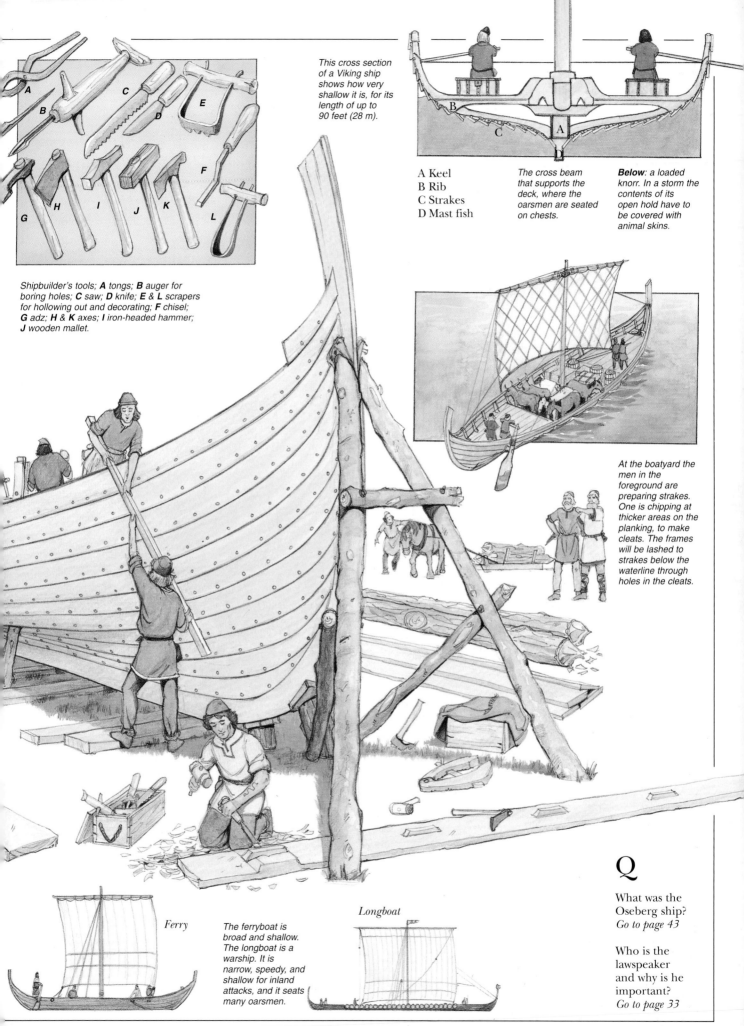

This cross section of a Viking ship shows how very shallow it is, for its length of up to 90 feet (28 m).

A Keel
B Rib
C Strakes
D Mast fish

The cross beam that supports the deck, where the oarsmen are seated on chests.

Below: a loaded knorr. In a storm the contents of its open hold have to be covered with animal skins.

Shipbuilder's tools; **A** tongs; **B** auger for boring holes; **C** saw; **D** knife; **E** & **L** scrapers for hollowing out and decorating; **F** chisel; **G** adz; **H** & **K** axes; **I** iron-headed hammer; **J** wooden mallet.

At the boatyard the men in the foreground are preparing strakes. One is chipping at thicker areas on the planking, to make cleats. The frames will be lashed to strakes below the waterline through holes in the cleats.

Ferry

The ferryboat is broad and shallow. The longboat is a warship. It is narrow, speedy, and shallow for inland attacks, and it seats many oarsmen.

Longboat

Q

What was the Oseberg ship?
Go to page 43

Who is the lawspeaker and why is he important?
Go to page 33

MERCHANTS

WHAT CAN YOU SELL?

IF YOU OWNED a trading boat, you were able to increase your fortune by bringing back goods from foreign lands to sell at home. You could share a boat with a group of companions and make your plans together. You might decide to go to one of the big Viking trading cities – Hedeby, for instance – where one met merchants bringing luxury goods from the south – fine textiles and tableware, jewelry and glass, Frankish swords, and Rhenish wine.

You could sail even farther northeast along the Baltic coast to get furs, ropes made of walrus hide, walrus ivory, and slaves. The slaves were captives who had been seized in the surrounding Slav lands. Your companions would help you to round up some, whom you would sell at a profit by taking them south along the Russian rivers.

Viking river routes led from the Baltic Sea to the Black Sea and the Caspian Sea.

Leaving Staraja Ladoga, you sail upstream in small boats laden with slaves, honey, wax, and furs to sell.

When you reach the river's source you drag the boats overland to get to another river flowing south.

You reach Kiev, where many Vikings have settled, and you trade with Arabs bringing silks and spices from the south.

You may seek your fortune even farther down to the Black Sea, and on to the splendid city of Constantinople.

Q

What is a byre, and what would you put in it?
Go to page 23

Why has your neighbor hung fish up outside his house?
Go to page 24

A SLAVE'S FATE

A Slav or Celtic family is captured by Viking raiders.

Men and women are led in chains to the Viking boats.

The Church may pay for captured Christians to save them.

On trading trips, slaves are useful to do the hard work.

Slaves can be bartered for goods in foreign lands.

Or sold in Viking markets, like Hedeby, for home use.

R A I D E R S
WOULD YOU MAKE A FORTUNE?

The earl and his men form a raiding fellowship. They swear loyalty to one another.

YOUR COMPANIONS could have suggested a much more exciting way of getting rich quickly. They had heard that a powerful earl in your area had just returned from a raiding party in one of the Christian lands over the sea. The people of these lands were wealthy, it seemed, with plenty of gold, silver, and fine furnishings in their houses, which could easily be taken from them in a quick surprise attack. Monasteries were good defenseless targets that provided rich pickings – holy goblets, garments, and richly jeweled boxes for storing relics and books. The earl was planning to raid again soon, and was looking for supporters to join him. Last time, his followers returned laden with treasure, as well as Christian slaves. Encampments in the Anglo-Saxon and Frankish lands were set up so that raids could be launched from a fixed base. A strong leader could take over large areas of land, which would provide good farming for Viking settlers.

Surprise is your strong point. The shallow ships go far upriver, enabling you to pounce on inland towns.

Each man brings his own fighting gear – sword, spear, shield, broadax, and helmet.

SOME OBJECTS found in Scandinavia that were probably seized as booty on raids: **a.** a Scottish or Irish reliquary looted to make a jewel box; **b.** a silver dish that was formerly a sacred church vessel; **c.** a bookmark used as a brooch; **d.** a gold scabbard end and belt end, both of Celtic workmanship.

Landing is easy anywhere. The boat is run ashore and everyone leaps out as soon as the keel scrapes the ground.

You will have to be ruthless when foreigners beg you not to kill them.

The ships were built so that both people and horses could get on and off them easily.

Local horses are seized in order to load the booty, round up slaves, and gallop back to the waiting ships.

The ship would tilt gracefully to one side to let the animals off, yet would remain stable and afloat.

Q

Your ship is caught in a storm. Whom can you turn to for help?
Go to page 36

You are wounded by a desperate Anglo-Saxon farmer.

You are helped away. What will happen to you next?

Your cousin, who is sarcastic, says something scornful to an acquaintance, who draws a sword and kills him.

You rush to tell his parents. The family discuss whether or not to accept payment for the wrong. They decide on revenge.

They kill a relative of the killer. In return, your father is killed because he is head of your cousin's family.

After many months of killing, the families let judges settle the dispute and decide the compensation.

Q

You are a farmer and have some livestock you want to sell. Where should you go?
Go to page 25

RIGHT AND WRONG
W H O   D E C I D E S ?

THE VIKING CODE OF HONOR was very strict. You had to obey it or you were despised by everyone. The most important rule was to be fearless and loyal. Nothing was lower than treachery. You supported your family or your leader without weighing the rights and wrongs of the matter.

Quarreling families could soon find themselves involved in a blood feud, as each sought vengeance by killing members of the other. The feud might end in a house burning. The men of one clan surprised the members of a family belonging to another in their home, surrounded the house, and set it on fire, giving the people inside the choice of burning to death or coming out and having all their menfolk slaughtered.

GROUNDS FOR divorce: blood ties are more important than those of marriage. One woman divorced her husband because he was friendly with her brother's killer.

VIKING VALUES

Honor. There is no deeper disgrace than being a coward. You must be ready to fight anyone who speaks ill of you or your family. You must support the lord to whom you have sworn loyalty. You must never surrender, but fight with your comrades until the end.

Generosity. Kings and earls reward their followers with gifts, for to give freely is the sign of a noble spirit. Even the poorest person would be ashamed to be stingy. You must welcome travelers and give them food, shelter, and protection. You may need the same one day.

Vigilance. Danger is never far away. The river may flood: pirates may attack: neighbors may seek revenge: there may be foreign enemies in the land. You will not last long unless you are ready for all comers. There is a saying: the wise man is never parted from his weapons.

WOMEN CANNOT speak at the Thing, but whole families come to the big annual meeting and camp while it lasts.

THE LAW IS not written down. Each year the Lawspeaker recites a third of it, so that people remember it.

YOU CAN TRADE and enjoy sport at the Thing. Wrestling and horsefighting are popular.

BANISHMENT OF ERIC THE RED

In 982, Eric the Red, an Icelandic settler from Norway, quarrels with a nearby farmer and kills him.

He is brought before the Thing. Thirty-six judges hear his case and banish him for three years.

He goes fishing and exploring with some friends. They find a land mostly frozen over, and spend the time there.

He names it Greenland, to persuade others to join him there. In 986, the first storm-tossed settlers arrive.

Apart from their feuding the Vikings were not lawless. They accepted the authority of traditional laws. Legal decisions were made by the freemen of the district at a meeting called the Thing. Judges imposed penalties for wrongdoing, based on a scale of payments. The highest was for killing a man, a lesser sum for chopping off his nose, and so on. Though judgment was made by the Thing, it was up to you to make the offender pay up. If you were bringing a lawsuit, you needed to take friends along to back you up. Decisions tended to be made in favor of the more powerful side. It paid to be the follower of a strong chief; he would support you.

Comradeship. Friends swear to be loyal to each other with a solemn oath by clasping hands. Such an oath makes them as close as members of your family. Groups of friends clasp hands to form a fellowship for a joint purpose – a raid, perhaps.

Ruthlessness. You do not spare enemies who would destroy you if they could. You do not rear sickly babies who may become sickly adults. Once, when there was a famine in Iceland, the old and the sick were thrown over cliffs. You cannot afford to be kind.

Rough Justice. Disagreements can be settled by a fight. Whoever wins is thought to have had right on his side. Duels, fought with swords and shields, are held where three roads meet. Wooden shields splinter easily, so each contestant is allowed three.

Q

What did the Arabs think of the way the Vikings lived?
Go to page 38

RIGHT AND WRONG 33

Overland travel is easier in winter, when horse-drawn sleds can glide easily over the snow.

You will have to use skis if you are going any distance on foot, or you may sink into a snowdrift.

Skaters strap lengths of bone to their shoes and push themselves along the frozen rivers with spiked sticks.

To make it easy to move goods, carts and sleds have removable bodies that can be loaded onto boats.

Q

Did the Vikings have a code of honor?
Go to pages 32-33

You've heard a story about someone who was killed by a spear of mistletoe. Can this be true?
Go to page 37

People travel on horseback if they can afford it. There are a few good roads and bridges on important routes.

Most rivers have to be forded at shallow points. These are sometimes marked by standing stones.

Carts are used to carry goods. Women may travel in them but men like to ride horses.

TRAVELING
HOW WOULD YOU TRAVEL?

AS A VIKING, YOU might have had to make some long journeys. You needed to know how to ride, ski, and skate, and how to handle a boat, a cart, and a sled. Men often left home on long trips, and came back with booty, bought or stolen. But there were some journeys from which people did not expect to return. Like it or not, you might have to leave your homeland. When your father died, your eldest brother took over the farm. If there was no land to spare, or you could not afford to buy any, you had to seek a new country, perhaps on the very edge of the world. The people below are setting off from Norway for a new life in Iceland. They are taking waterproof skins and food for the journey, which may last more than a week, tools for metalworking and carpentry, animals for their farms, and slaves.

SAILING WEST

How will you know in which direction to sail when you are at sea? You do not have a compass to tell you which way your boat is pointing; the Vikings did not know about the magnetic north. Whenever possible, you keep the coast in sight and look out for well-known landmarks.

On the open sea you will have to watch the position of the sun or the stars. When the sun seems highest, it is due south. This high point will be closer to the horizon the farther north you sail. By measuring this distance, you will be able to judge how far north you are.

There are many other signs that may help you to judge a ship's position. Cloud formations and the flight of seabirds can show that land is just over the horizon. Alterations in the waves suggest changes of depth, and the presence of currents and underwater rocks.

On the long voyage to a new home, you have to sleep wherever you can, huddled under skins. There is no shelter in storms.

As the boat nears land, you throw overboard the posts of your high seat. They will guide you to your new home.

At your journey's end, you search for a sheltered landing place. Then you unload and lead out the animals.

LANDING

One of the first things you will want is a hot meal. It has not been possible to cook on board ship.

Left: finds that prove the sagas have some truth.

A Viking pin and spindle whorl found in Newfoundland, and an American Indian arrowhead discovered in Greenland.

You will have to live in a tent at first. If you have not brought one, you can use timber and animal skins.

Above: the Icelanders, who settled in Greenland and found America, came largely from Norway.

Following the will of the gods, you make the new farm on the spot where the posts you threw overboard have come ashore.

At first the native Americans were friendly. The skraelings, as the Vikings called them, were pleased to part with furs of fine quality in return for pieces of red cloth.

Aud the Deep-Minded, a widowed noblewoman, led her dependents to Iceland and handed out land like a chief.

You would have heard many tales of the heroes who sailed west. They discovered Iceland in about 860. The fishing there was so good that the first settlers did little else. Because they forgot to make hay, their cattle died of starvation in the winter and they had to return to Norway. The families that went there later were wiser. They made successful farms in the grassy areas. Unfortunately, there was soon not enough to go around. People were forced to look further, to harsh, treeless Greenland, and even beyond.

The sagas say America was sighted in 986 by a man called Bjarni, who had been blown off course on his way to Greenland. Wanting to reach his goal, he did not go ashore. In about 1000, Leif the Lucky, son of Eric the Red, bought Bjarni's boat and, following his directions, reached the unknown land.

He arrived somewhere in the region of Labrador and sailed south until he came to a land with rich grass and waters full of salmon. He decided to spend the winter there and sent his crew exploring. One man rushed back with amazing news. He had found grapes growing wild!

When Leif came home with news of this land, many Greenlanders were eager to settle there. Several attempts were made, including one led by a man named Thorfinn. His followers spent three years there, but the natives grew hostile and forced the out-numbered Vikings to leave.

Q

Where would you look for Asgard and the world serpent?
Go to page 8

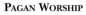

RELIGION
WHAT DO YOU BELIEVE?

A S A VIKING, you had to decide whether or not to become a Christian. The Vikings worshiped many gods. The Christians had only one god, but to judge from the prosperity of Christian countries and the splendor of their churches, this god was very powerful. You would have heard of him from Vikings who had been abroad, or perhaps from Frankish missionaries. You might have wanted to add this Christian god to the Viking ones, but the missionaries did not like that. Merchants found that it paid to be Christian, for Christians like to trade with other Christians.

You could compromise by letting them make the sign of the cross over you. This was not a proper baptism so you could still worship your own gods, but it made you Christian enough to do business with.

Animals are sacrificed to the gods at festivals. People put their offerings on poles outside their houses.

Local chiefs lead the worship in their own houses or outdoors, in sacred groves of trees.

Thor the thunder god is friendly to humans. You can call on his help in an emergency, as this sailor is doing.

Frey ensures prosperity and makes humans and animals fertile. Wedding toasts are drunk in his honor.

Q

Why would anyone want to bury a ship?
Go to page 41

You are a slave and you've just been bought. What kind of life will you have?
Go to pages 15, 30, and 31

If you bow down with gifts before images of the gods, they may grant your wishes. Ibn Fadlan saw Viking traders doing this.

A small bronze figure of the god Frey, found in Sweden. He wears a pointed cap, and is seated cross-legged, and tugs at his beard.

This little figure of a woman holding a drinking horn may represent a Valkyrie, a fierce female spirit. It is probably an amulet.

The metalworker who used this soapstone mold wanted to be sure of customers. It casts both crosses and Thor's hammer.

Left: a fabulous beast forming a post end that was probably part of a chair. It was found in the Oseberg ship burial. Such figures may have been meant to frighten off evil spirits.

A figure of Odin from a Vendel helmet (from earlier Viking times). He is shown as a warrior accompanied by an eagle and a raven.

Warriors in the carving below seem to be making an offering to Odin. Three triangles are his symbol.

Left: amulet in the form of Thor's hammer.

Greenland's first church, built by the wife of Eric the Red.

THE COMING OF CHRISTIANITY

The first missionaries were allowed to build churches, but their bell-ringing was not popular.

If you decide to be baptized, you will be given new clothes, the symbol of a new life. Some people are baptized several times!

Harald Bluetooth, king of Denmark, is said to have been converted on seeing a bishop miraculously hold a bar of white-hot iron in his hand.

FIERCE FEMALE SPIRITS called Valkyries hover over the battlefield and take the slain to Asgard, where they are welcomed with horns full of ale.

THREE SISTERS WITH covered faces sit by a well beneath one of the roots of Yggdrasil. They are the Norns, the spirits who spin the thread of life and death.

Many stories are told of kindly but hot-tempered Thor. Once he went fishing and almost succeeded in catching the terrible world serpent.

TALES FROM THE SAGAS

The mysterious god Odin gave the gift of poetry and the magic of runes to the world. He lost an eye in his search for wisdom.

The pagan gods were still remembered in Christian times, in stories told around the fireside, and in old songs the skalds sang. A skald was a professional poet kept by a Viking chief. His job was to entertain at feasts and to proclaim his employer's brave deeds in verse, so that they would never be forgotten. The verses tell of Odin's realm, Gladsheim, and of his eight-legged horse, Sleipnir, of Thor's mighty hammer, of the hero Sigurd the dragon-slayer, and many other tales.

Silver filigree cross from a grave at Birka, Sweden.

Pendant that can be either Thor's hammer or a cross, depending on which way it is worn.

Frigg is the wife of Odin. She has a palace of her own, where she sits spinning thread to weave into clouds.

The spiteful Loki often changes shape. When he was a mare, he gave birth to Odin's eight-legged horse.

Balder, whom all the gods loved, was killed by a spear of mistletoe, through a trick of evil Loki.

Q

If you wanted to wash your clothes, why might a cow come in handy?
Go to page 21

If you were a slave, where would you eat your meals?
Go to page 15

In the year 1000, Icelanders attending the Thing are ready to come to blows over whether or not the whole nation should become Christian.

The Lawspeaker lies in his tent all day and all night, considering. Then he urges the Vikings to be Christian and worship as they wish in private.

This satisfies everyone. Many are baptized at once, but some say the water is too cold. They want to wait until they reach their local hot springs.

YOUR HEALTH
HOW DO YOU KEEP CLEAN AND WELL?

The bathhouse is a separate stone-floored building with a drain, and a fire on which stones are heated.

When the stones are red-hot, water is thrown on them, filling the room with steam. Then you swelter in the heat.

If you like it very hot, you can sit on the bench along the wall and whip yourself with a bundle of twigs.

This opens the pores and makes you sweat. To tone up, you should then go outside and roll in the snow.

THE VIKINGS HAD A MIXED reputation for cleanliness, depending on whose opinion you accept. The English learned to get on reasonably well with the Danes who had settled in their land, but they thought they washed too much. They combed their hair a lot, had a bath once a week, and changed their underclothes frequently. The English thought that this was obviously a scheme to win the most attractive Anglo-Saxon women.

The Arab, Ibn Fadlan, who met the Vikings on the river Volga, formed a very different impression. They were as dirty as stray donkeys, he reported. They did not wash after going to the bathroom or after a meal. Arabs were used to very high standards of cleanliness. Their civilization was much more advanced than that of Europe, so there is no reason to think that the Vikings were less fussy than their neighbors. In fact, the Viking name for Saturday means bath day.

ABOVE ARE the remains of a wooden toilet seat found during the excavation of the Viking town at York. On the right is a suggestion of the sort of toilet you might find it in. The seat goes over a hole in the ground or over a bucket. You may be the one who has to empty this.

Many Viking combs have been found. Women certainly needed them for their long hair, which was worn in a knot.

Travel could be dirty and tiring. Guests should be greeted with water, a towel, and a hearty welcome.

They are given time to wash and refresh themselves, some dry clothes, and a place by the fire.

The English disapproved of a Danish hairstyle that was very short at the neck and had long bangs.

WASHING

Q

You've decided to become a shipwright. How can you find out more about it?
Go to pages 28-29

An Arab traveling along the Volga described some Viking traders washing. He was disgusted by them.

He says that he saw a woman slave bring a bowl of water in which the first man washed his face and hair.

Then the man sneezed and blew his nose into the water before handing the bowl to the next person.

The bowl was passed from man to man until each had washed his hair, and blown his nose in the same water.

An Arab traveling in Russia noticed that when Viking men needed to urinate they went out in groups of four, with their hands on their swords, to protect each other.

Ibn Fadlan also thought poorly of Viking medical skills. This was not surprising, as Arab doctors were then the best in the world, apart from the Chinese. If you were wounded in battle you were bandaged and treated with herb poultices, but if these did not work, people did not linger at your bedside. When Vikings saw that action was unlikely to get results, they did not waste time on it. Illnesses were treated with traditional plant recipes, but spells and amulets were also thought to be very effective. Runes were believed to have magical powers. They were carved on pieces of bone and put beneath a sick person's pillow and written on the palms of women during childbirth.

Studies of Viking skeletons show that many people suffered from wear and tear in the joints. They also prove that, as a Viking, your teeth will be worn to stumps by eating bread full of grit from the quern stones. However, this will not hurt, and your teeth will not decay because you do not eat sweets. There is no sugar!

A VIKING DIAGNOSIS

Your raiding party meets fierce resistance. An unexpected spear pierces your chest.

You are carried back to the camp where your wound is washed and you are given onion porridge to eat.

The porridge will help your companions to decide whether there is any hope of your getting better.

If they can smell onions through the wound they will know that the stomach has been pierced and you will die.

Combs with very fine teeth like this suggest that the Vikings might have found head lice a problem.

A scoop for cleaning the ears.

ICELANDERS HAVE extra encouragement to wash, as their land has volcanic hot springs. The hot-water bathing pool that Snorri Sturluson made at his farm at Reykholt is still there today.

Q

Do you know where slaves come from? *Go to pages 30-31*

Everybody is talking about the Thing. What is it? *Go to page 33*

TREATING THE SICK

The same Arab observer describes the way in which the Vikings he met treat someone who becomes ill.

They put the sick person in a tent by himself. This might have been a precaution against infection.

The invalid is left alone with some bread and water so that he has something to eat and drink if he feels strong enough.

Apart from this, he gets hardly any attention. If he is a slave he is left entirely by himself.

If the sick man is lucky enough to recover, he rejoins his companions. If he dies, his body is burned.

A slave is not thought to be worth burning. His body is left in the open to be eaten by dogs or vultures.

FROM CRADLE TO GRAVE
BIRTH, MARRIAGE, AND DEATH

Your mother is looked after by the women of the house. They wash you and take you to your father.

BIRTHS WERE always welcomed in a Viking family. Young people guaranteed the family's future survival. Vikings celebrated births and weddings with feasting and much ale drinking. Old age was not a time of life to be celebrated. In a cold climate, where hard work was needed to make crops grow and animals thrive, frail old people were a burden to their families. Although not actively cruel to the old, the Vikings did not regard them as a blessing. Women who survived the dangers of childbirth could live to over fifty. Men faced many perils and did not expect to live as long.

An ordinary person's grave. The body is placed directly in the earth in a wood-lined pit.

You are a strong, healthy baby and he is delighted. He sprinkles you with water and gives you a name.

This means that he accepts you into the family. But if you are sickly, he may not think you are worth rearing.

Horses slaughtered

If so, he may tell a servant to leave you in some exposed place where you will not survive long.

YOUR DEATH

Q

If someone insulted your family, what could you do about it?
Go to page 32

Above: *the funeral of a Viking chief, one of the leaders of the Viking traders in Russia. It was watched by an Arab traveler on the Volga in 922. This is what he tells his fellow travelers.*

One of the dead man's slave women must volunteer to die with him.

For ten days she is waited on by two attendants. She drinks and sings.

The chief lies in a temporary grave, while special clothes are made for him.

On the day of the funeral, his boat is hauled ashore onto a pile of wood.

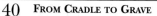

A tent is set up in the boat, and it is spread with rugs and cushions.

Left: this large ship burial must be for a rich man's funeral. A less important person might by buried in a small boat, or a boat-shaped grave marked by stones.

Below: the chief's followers set light to the ship. An old woman known as the Angel of Death carries away the dagger with which she has killed the slave.

YOU ARE MARRIED

The groom pays a "bride-price" to his wife. He gets her dowry, but must return it if she leaves him.

The most noble death was to die in battle. A "straw death," which meant dying of old age on your mattress, was despised. Those who died on the battlefield joined Odin, the god of warriors, in his hall, Valhalla. Their bodies were either burned or buried, according to the custom of their region. The objects that they needed in the afterlife were placed beside them. Women joined Frigg in her hall.

If you were the slave of a rich master or mistress, you might have been chosen to die with them, an honor that was difficult to refuse. However, this was not a custom followed by all Vikings and was certainly not practiced by Vikings who were Christians.

The couple join hands and drink bridal ale before witnesses, who must lead the man to his wife's bed.

If you are not happy with your husband you can get a divorce by declaring the fact before witnesses.

A dissatisfied husband can do the same. He can treat his women servants and slaves as wives.

Angel of Death

Q

You have to feed your family. How can you bake some bread?
Go to page 18

The corpse is dug up, dressed in splendid clothes, and put in the tent.

Two horses, two cows, a dog, a cock, and a hen are killed and put with him.

The slave is lifted to look over a frame. She says she sees Paradise beyond.

She is led onto the ship, drinks a strong beverage and sings farewell, and is killed.

The ship is set ablaze. The nearest kinsman starts the fire.

A post bearing the dead man's name is set on the mound covering his ashes.

This Swedish rune stone records that Ulv from Uppland went raiding three times in England, and got a share in the silver taken.

TO HELP US FIND out about the Vikings, we have, first of all, their own messages to us on over 2,700 rune stones. These were put up to commemorate Viking people and their deeds. There are also the writings of people who lived at the time when the Vikings were active. Christian monks and Arab travelers have left vivid accounts of the Vikings as raiders and traders. Christian histories of the lives of kings and churchmen often refer to Viking lands. The Icelandic sagas, written more than two centuries after Viking times, have much to tell, though their picture of daily life in what was by then a bygone age may not be entirely accurate.

A lion, now in Venice, received Viking graffiti when at its former site near Athens.

ALFRED THE GREAT, king of Wessex in England, recorded that a Norwegian chieftain called Ohthere visited his court in 890. He came from the far north where the Lapps of Lapland paid him tribute with furs, reindeer hides, walrus ivory, and ropes made of skin.

THE VIKING FUNERAL described on pages 40 and 41 was witnessed on the river Volga by an Arab whose name was Ibn Fadlan.

He was acting as ambassador for the caliph of Baghdad. An account of his journey appears in an Arab book of geography.

Adam of Bremen, a German monk, wrote a history of the archbishops of Hamburg, in about 1075. It has much to tell about Viking lands and way of life.

The sagas, first written down in the thirteenth century, are traditional stories of Viking kings and heroes. Many were collected by the scholar Snorri Sturluson.

Archaeologists have found traces of Viking towns, farmsteads, and burial sites. Objects of metal, glass, and ceramics, which last well in the ground, show us the weapons, jewelry, and tools people used. Human bones may reveal the diseases people had, how long they lived, and how they died.

A man's grave discovered at Birka in Sweden. The objects buried with him included his sword, ax, spear, and a bronze dish.

The pagan custom of providing a corpse with valued possessions, food, and tools to use in the afterlife has given us much information.

HOW DO WE KNOW?

The excavation of the Oseberg ship. The objects it contained had been preserved by airtight conditions within the mound. Lengthy exposure to air causes wood to decay. Contrary to what you might expect, water also preserves it. Sunken ships and remains found in waterlogged sites (Hedeby, for instance) have lasted well.

SCIENTIFIC analysis of refuse tells us about hygiene and diet, and timber may help to date a site through a process called dendro-chronology. The yearly rings of growth in trees vary in width, and wood of the same age shows the same variation. Timber can be dated if its rings match those in wood of a known date.

The Oseberg ship was old when it was buried. It can be dated by the style of the carving on its stem and sternpost.

Below: Arab coins, found in hoards of Viking silver buried for safekeeping, show the extent of trade with the south.

The burial was lavish, including beds and bedding, kitchen things, looms, a cart, and four sleds, three splendidly carved.

The Oseberg burial mound had originally been 20 ft (6 m) high and over 120 ft (36 m) across. The ship was moored to a large stone within it. The corpses had been placed in a grave chamber in the stern.
Archaeologists have established that the burial dates from the second half of the ninth century. Plant traces prove that it took place in August or September.

Goods buried with the Vikings give clues about their religious beliefs. Among the most spectacular Viking finds are two boat burials discovered in Norway, one at Gokstad in 1880 and the other at Oseberg in 1903. Previously, it had been assumed the Viking ships were quite clumsily built. These vessels, both over 70 feet (21 m) long, transformed people's knowledge of Viking skills.

The Oseberg ship, built around 800, seems to have been a pleasure boat made for shallow waters. A young woman had been buried in it, together with an elderly attendant and a host of objects that they might have needed.

The Gokstad ship, circa 850, was a more strongly built boat. It contained the bones of a man, twelve horses, six dogs, and a peacock, as well as many personal objects and three rowing boats. A copy was built and it sailed successfully to America in 1893. Parts of the Viking towns hidden under modern York and Dublin have been excavated recently, and an entire village has been uncovered at Vorbasse in Denmark.

Replicas of ships have been tried out at sea to test speed, steering, and rigging.

Diving to examine the wrecks of five Viking boats found in Roskilde fjord in Denmark. They were located in 1957.

The boats had been deliberately sunk to make a barrier across the fjord. One was a longboat 92 feet (28 m) in length.

Archaeology in the laboratory (below right). Under the microscope, tiny particles of matter can yield secrets. At York, for instance, parasite remains proved that some Vikings suffered from intestinal worms.

The Vikings have left us few portraits. This head from Sweden shows a trimly bearded warrior.

TIMESPAN

AT THE DAWN OF THE VIKING age, there were three great powers in the western world: the Franks, who ruled what is now France and Germany; the Byzantines, who had inherited the eastern half of the Roman Empire; and the Arabs, whose civilization extended from western Asia, through North Africa to Spain. Most of Europe, including Britain and Ireland, was Christian by this time, though the Scandinavians and the Slavs of eastern Europe were still pagan.

The Scandinavians were already prosperous traders in the areas around the Baltic Sea. Before 700, the Swedes had expanded eastward, setting up colonies along the Baltic coast. At the end of the eighth century, the Norwegians made the first of what were to be repeated Viking attacks on countries to the west. No one knows for certain what caused these attacks, but it was probably a combination of greed for riches, and the need to find new land, as rising population created a shortage at home. Some settlers may have had a political motive in not wanting to submit to increasingly powerful kings.

793 Norwegian Vikings attack and destroy the monastery on the island of Lindisfarne, which is off the Northumbrian coast of England. England at this time is divided into several small kingdoms, of which Mercia, Wessex, East Anglia, and Northumbria are the most important. There is no royal authority that is strong enough to organize a successful defense against these attacks.

795 They attack St. Columba's monastery at Iona in western Scotland, and raid the coast of Wales. C.800, Norwegian Vikings land in the Orkney and Shetland Isles, and the Faroes. These provide a base for raids on Ireland.

810 King Godfred of Denmark invades neighboring Frisia.

828 Irish chroniclers record that their country is overrun by Viking pirates.

834 Danes attack and raid the Frisian trading center at Dorestad on the Rhine, and begin to launch regular attacks on the lands of the Franks.

835 The Danes attack Sheppey, an island at the mouth of the Thames, in England.

841 Norwegian Vikings begin to settle permanently in Ireland, and Dublin is founded. Ireland serves as a starting point for the colonization of the Isle of Man, southwestern Scotland, and northwestern England. In the same year, the Danes sail up the Seine and attack and raid Rouen.

843 The Danes sail up the Loire River in France and attack Nantes. They destroy towns and monasteries all over western France. The terrified peasants flee, and the land is laid waste.

844 Vikings capture Seville in Spain, but only manage to hold it for a week as the Arabs soon put them to flight.

845 Paris in France, and Hamburg in Germany are attacked and plundered. Charles the Bald, who is king of the West Franks, pays the first of many large payments, known as Danegeld. This was used by the rulers to try to buy off the Vikings and stop their attacks.

850 Danes begin to stay the winter in England.

859 A fleet of ships enters the Mediterranean, where the Vikings raid for three years, spending the winter on an island in the Rhone. They attack Spain, southern France, North Africa, and Italy. They sack Pisa.

860-874 The first settlers arrive in Iceland.

864 Charles the Bald forbids the sale of weapons or horses to the Vikings.

865 A large Viking force lands in England, seeking land to settle.

866 The force captures York. By the early 870s, Vikings control most of eastern England. They begin to share out the land. A further expansion is defeated by Alfred, king of Wessex, who makes Viking leaders accept Christianity.

886 A treaty between Alfred and Guthrum defines the frontier of the Danelaw. Alfred's successors gradually regain control in England, though the Viking settlers remain.

891 Vikings are defeated by the Franks. Frankish defenses are well organized and the Viking threat grows weaker on the continent.

911 Rollo is given Normandy by King Charles the Simple in exchange for a promise to defend France from other Vikings. Throughout the tenth century Swedish Vikings are active along trade routes in Russia.

C.960 Harald Bluetooth, king of Denmark, converts his country to Christianity.

980 A new wave of Viking attacks and raids on England begins.

C.986 Eric the Red goes to Greenland.

991 The English pay the first in a new series of Danegeld.

994 A fleet of 94 ships, led by Olaf Tryggvason of Norway and Svein Forkbeard of Denmark, attacks London.

995 Olaf, the Christian king of Norway, makes his people convert.

C.1000 Leif Eriksson leaves Greenland to look for land to the west.

1009 Chief Thorkel the Tall ravages England for three years and extorts 48,000 pounds of silver.

1013 Svein returns, and by 1017 controls all of England. His son Canute rules until 1035. Canute gains control of Norway and Sweden, and is also ruler of Denmark.

1042 The accession of an English king, Edward the Confessor, ends Danish rule in England.

1066 The Norwegian king Harald Hardrada invades England and is killed in battle at Stamford Bridge, near York. He is the last great Viking ruler.

C.1100 Close of the Viking age as Viking settlers become absorbed into local populations.

1406-10 Icelanders visiting Greenland report back that Viking desendants are still to be found there. By the sixteenth century only the native Inuit people remain.

Q1 If you heard that someone had lost half his quern, would you think he was having difficulty

A thinking straight
B making bread
C finding his way at sea

Q2 Thor is the name of

A the season when the snow melts
B the thunder god
C the town founded by Godfred of Denmark

Q3 Greenland is so called because its

A discoverers thought it needed an attractive name
B its snow looks greenish in the distance
C it was discovered by Erik the Green

Q4 Your knorr is over-loaded. Is it likely to

A capsize
B refuse to go at more than a walking pace
C reveal what a greedy eater you are

Q5 The Norns are

A three dangerous rocks off the Orkneys
B three mysterious women
C three giants

Q6 Bjarni is the name of

A the god who was killed by a spear of mistletoe
B the man who missed the chance to be the first European in America
C the bishop who converted Harald Bluetooth

Q7 Sleipner is the name of

A Odin's horse
B Thor's hammer
C the world serpent

Q8 Skraeling is the Viking term for

A a person you think is a savage
B a coarse cloth you think is fit only for slaves
C a wad of animal hair used in caulking boats

Q9 Tablet weaving is

A an interwoven pattern found only on rune stones
B a way of making checked ribbon
C a way of making patterned ribbon

Q10 Canute was

A the discoverer of Iceland
B the king of England
C the man killed by Eric the Red

Q11 Vikings remember Sigurd because he killed

A a famous dragon
B a famous missionary
C a Frankish king

Q12 You have been spending time at the shieling. Have you been

A steering a boat
B judging a family dispute
C grazing cattle

Q13 Soapstone is

A a large rock near a river, on which clothes are scrubbed
B a soft rock from which bowls are carved
C a semiprecious stone used by bead makers

Q14 Dendro-chronology is

A the method used to assess the probable speed of Viking boats
B the term for an early way of telling the time
C a technique for dating objects made of wood

Q15 A skald is

A a Viking entertainer
B a Viking dagger
C a Viking drinking toast

TO FIND OUT what your survival rating is, *go to page 48.*

GLOSSARY

AMULET a small object, either worn or carried, which was thought to ward off evil.

BOG IRON lumps of iron ore, which are found in marshy ground.

BYRE a cow barn.

CALIPH the title given to the supreme ruler of the Moslems.

CARNELIAN a reddish semiprecious stone.

CAULKING tarred animal hair put between the side planking of a boat to make it watertight.

CLEATS small pieces of wood fastened to, or left projecting from, the timbers of a ship.

COPPICE to cut back young shrubs or trees regularly, so that they form thickets of slender stems.

DAMASCENING the process of fusing iron and steel to produce a wavy pattern.

DAUB a mixture of mud and straw.

DISTAFF a long cleft stick, on which a spinner holds the wool or flax about to be spun.

FILIGREE an openwork decoration on jewelry, made of gold or silver wire and tiny balls of gold or silver.

GRIDDLE a metal support with a handle, used for cooking bread, cakes, etc., over a fire.

GROUNDWATER water that collects naturally some distance below ground.

KEEL the lowest, lengthwise timber of a boat, on which the sides are built up.

MAGNETIC behaving as a magnet. The earth is a magnet. Its poles will attract a magnetized compass needle.

MISSIONARY a Christian sent to another country to convert its people to Christianity.

PAGAN belonging to a faith that is not Christian.

ROVE a small metal plate over which the protruding end of a nail is bent and hammered flat.

RUNES Viking alphabet. Letters used for casting spells and writing.

SADDLERY saddles and other leather equipment for horses.

STARBOARD the right-hand side of a boat.

STAVE a thin, narrow piece of wood.

VALHALLA Viking Heaven.

VALKYRIES Odin's nine daughters, and fierce female spirits of Viking legend.

VENDEL belonging to Scandinavian culture of the two centuries before the Viking age, named after finds made at Vendel, Sweden.

VENISON deer meat.

WARP THREADS threads that run lengthwise in woven material. In an upright loom, they hang down. Weft threads are woven across them.

YEASTS microscopic fungi, often used for baking bread.

INDEX

Page numbers in bold refer to illustrations.

A

Adam of Bremen 42, **42**
Alfred the Great (King of Wessex) 42, **42**, 45
America 8, 35
animal sacrifice 36
Arabs 38
archaeology 42, 43

B

Balder 37, **37**
bathhouse 38, **38**
bathing 38, **38**
Birka 42
birth 40, **40**
Bjarni 35, **35**
blacksmith 11, 26, **26**
bread, making 10, 18, **18**
brooches 21
making 20, **20**
burial 41
burial boats 41, **41**
Gokstad and Oseberg 36, 43, **43**

C

children 11, 14, **14**
Christianity 36, 37, 44, 45
Christians 31, 41
missionaries 6, **15**, 47

claiming land 23, 35
cleanliness 38, 43
clothes 9, 10, 20-21, **20-21**
children's **21**
cleaning of **21**
getting dressed 20, **20**
ironing 20
making 12, 20-21, **26**
merchant's **21**
shoes **21**
coins 24, **24**, **43**
combs 39, **39**
crafts 27, **27**
antler comb 27, **27**
bone-carving 27, **27**
brooch-making 20, **20**
leather working 27, **27**
craftsmen 11, 24, 27

D

Danegeld 44, 45
Danes 44
death 40, 41
Denmark 6, 7, 8
diet 18, 43
divorce 32, 41

E

earls 15, **15**
England 6, 44, 45
Eric the Red 45
banishment of 33, **33**

F

Fadlan, Ibn 38, 39, 42
family 14

farmhouse **22**, 23, **23**
farming 7, 10, 22-23, **22-23**
byres 23, **23**, 47
claiming land 23
farmer's wife, life of 23, **23**
in Iceland 22-23, **22-23**
shieling 22, **22**
ferry longship 27
feuds 15, 32
fishing 6, 35
food 18-19, **18-19**
preparation 19
France 8, 44
Franks 44, 45
freemen 14, 15
Frey (god) 36
Frigg (wife of Odin) 37, **37**, 41
funeral, Viking 40-41, **40-41**
furniture 17

G, H

generosity 32
gods 8, 35, 36
Greenland 6, 8, 33, 35, 45, 46
first church in **36**

Harald Bluetooth (king of Denmark) 36, 45
Hedeby 24-25, **24-25**, 30
Hel 8
honor 14, 32-33
houses 10, 16-17, **16-17**
building 16, **16**

wattle and daub 17, **17**
wood 16
hunting 8, 18

I

Iceland 45
farmhouse in 16, **16**
illness 39
Ireland 8, 44, 45
iron 11, 26, 27

J, K

jewelry, making 27, **27**

king 15, **15**, **25**
knorr 28, **29**, 46

L

language (Old Norse) 7
laws 33
Lawspeaker 12, 33, 37, **37**
Leif the Lucky 35, **35**
Loki (evil god) 37, **37**

M

marriage 41, **41**
medecine 39
merchants 24, 25, 30, **30**
cloths of **21**
monasteries 31

N

names 9
Norns 37, **37**, 46
Norway 6, 7, 8, 35, 43
Norwegians 44

O, P

Odin 36, **36**, 37, **37**, 41
Olaf 14
old people 40

paganism 8, 36, 37, 42, 47

R

raids, Viking 8, 6, 31, **31**, 44
objects seized on a **31**
religion 6, 12, 36-37
runes 11, 39, 42, 47
Russia 8, 25, 30

S

sagas 35, 37, 42
sailing 28, 34
Scandinavia 6, 7, 44
Scotland 44
settlers, Viking 35
shieling 22, **22**
ship burial (see burial boats)
ships 28-29, **28-29**
shipbuilding 28-29, **28-29**
tools used **29**
shoes **21**
skald 37
skraelings (native Americans) 35, **35**
slaves 6, 15, **15**, **25**, 30
society 11, 15
Spain 44
Staraja Ladoga 25, **25**
storehouses 11, **17**

Sturluson, Snorri 39, 42, **42**
Sweden 6, 8, 9, 45
swords 26, **26**, 30

T

taxes 25
thatching 17, **17**
Thing, the 14, 15, 33, **33**, 37
Thor (thunder god) 36, 37, **37**, 46
toilet 24, 38, **38**
trade 8, 12, 24, 25, 30, 33
trading routes 30, **30**
travel 12, 34-35, **34-35**
by cart **34**
by sled **34**
finding direction 34, **34**
on horseback **34**
on skates **34**
on skis **34**

V

Valkyries 36, 37, **37**, 47
values 6, 32, 33

W, Y

washing 38, **38**, 39
weaving 26, **26**
women 14, **14**, 19, 26
clothes worn by 20, **20**
hairstyles 20, **38**
writing 7

York 38, 43, 45

ANSWERS

HAVE YOU SURVIVED?

Here are the quiz answers, with pages to turn to if you need an explanation.

Q	
1(B) - page 18	8(A) - page 35
2(B) - page 36	9(C) - page 26
3(A) - page 33	10(B) - page 45
4(A) - page 29	11(A) - page 37
5(B) - page 37	12(C) - page 22
6(B) - page 35	13(B) - page 27
7(A) - page 37	14(C) - page 43
	15(A) - page 37

Count up your correct answers and find out what your survival rating is.

14 - 15 Excellent! You could be a Viking chief.
11 - 13 You would make a good loyal follower of the chief.
6 -10 You might do better to stay at home by the fire.
5 - 0 Terrible! You would be sold as a slave!

ACKNOWLEDGMENTS
The Salariya Book Co Ltd would like to thank the following people for their assistance:

Sarah Ridley
Penny Clarke
Jenny Millington